Praise for *Roots Music: Listening to Jazz*

"Eve West Bessier's combination of alliteration and onomatopoeia frames some of the most colorful and inventive of either ever put together in the name of jazz."

    Gloria Krolak, Poetry Editor, *Jersey Jazz*

"A treasure chest of exuberance, playfulness, cleverness, and heart-break, each poem is inspired by and dedicated to a specific piece of jazz music. The musicality of the poems themselves is filled with riffs of alliteration, cheeky surprises, and melancholy caresses. Gorgeous imagery revels with astonishing glissandos of philosophy."

    Beate Sigriddaughter, Poet Laureate Emerita of Silver City, New Mexico. Author of *Xanthippe and Her Friends.*

"Eve West Bessier enacts the structures and sounds of jazz in an ekphrastic homage. These are poems with groove poems that bop, poems whose rhythms are as engaging and elusive as that quintessential jazz concept, swing. These musical and moving poems demand to be read aloud."

    Joshua McKinney, Ph.D. Author of *Small Sillion.*

Roots Music

Listening to Jazz

This is a work of poetic fiction. All of the characters, organizations, and events portrayed are either products of the author's imagination, or are used fictitiously.

Roots Music, Listening to Jazz, Copyright © 2019 Eve West Bessier. All rights reserved.

ISBN: 978-1-7338478-1-0 (trade paperback)

Published by Falcon West Books

10 9 8 7 6 5 4 3 2 1

Printed in the United States of America.

Cover design: Eve West Bessier

Also by Eve West Bessier

New Rain, a visionary novel, Spring 2019
Exposures: Tripod Poems, Fall 2019
Pink Cadillacs, short stories, Spring 2020

Roots Music

Listening to Jazz

Eve West Bessier

Falcon West Books

Acknowledgments

I extend my gratitude to the editors of the journals and anthologies in which the following poems included in this collection first appeared.

Blue Moon Literary and Art Review: "Death of the Bull"
North American Review: "Zoo You, Boogaloo"
Lyric: "After the Rain"
Americas Review: "Dos Gardenias Para Tí"
Kalliope: "The Love Tattoo"
Heart Flip (anthology): "More Sublime Need"
Riparian Writing (anthology): "Beneath the Surface," "Subterranean"

The following poems included in this collection received awards or honors.

"Death of the Bull," Second Place, The Jack Kerouac Contest, 2008
"Zoo You, Boogaloo," Pushcart Prize nomination, 2003
"Dos Gardenias Para Tí," First Prize, California Focus on Writers, 2000
"The Love Tattoo," The Kathryn Hohlwein Award, 2000

An earlier version of this collection received the honor of being Runner Up in the *Georgetown Review* Poetry Manuscript Contest in 2015.

*For Elisabeth and Patrick
with all my love*

Author's Note

Each poem in this collection was inspired by listening to live or recorded jazz.

The name and artist of the specific jazz composition that inspired each poem are listed beneath the poem's title.

Table of Contents

Bebop

All About the Music

Zoo You, Boogaloo	1
Jazz	2
Blue Hues	4
Off the Tip of Midnight	6
Salt Peanuts	8
Serengeti Sunrise	9
Set to Boil	10
Tuesdays and Fridays	11
Spin Doctor	12
Queen of Swing	13
Cornerstones	14
Unexpected	15
Audacious	16
Synthesis	18
Manic	20
Bolero Son	22
Phantom Cellophane	24
Calif-horn-ication	25

Straight, No Chaser

People, Places, and Traces

Calliope	29
Dos Gardenias Para Tí	30
Midnight Wages	32
After the Rain	34
Paris Before Dawn	35
Beneath the Surface	36
Jardín Rocoso	38
Seaside Lullaby	39
Ode to the Clarinet	40
Phoenix The Vegas Showgirl	42
Swank	44
Pintadas	45
Immobility	46
Jazz at Hoffman's	48
Ode to Chocolate	49
The Jib's Up	50
Pink Cadillac	51
Crossing the Golden Gate	52
Chaos Theory	54
Death of the Bull	56

West of the Moon

Ballads, Blues, and Ruminations

Façade	61
Gibbous Moon	62
In the House of Love	64
Dolphins Have No Furniture	65
More Sublime Need	66
Blues in B Minor	67
Tailings	68
Oklahoma Memory	70
And That Is Enough	72
The Love Tattoo	74
Circuitous Root	80
No Ground	82
Power Money	83
Subterranean	84
Wild Perfume	85
Begin Here	86
About the Author	89

Bebop

All About the Music

Zoo You, Boogaloo

(listening to "Freddy Freeloader" by Miles Davis)

Rhinos rubbin aphrodisiac horns, scopin the score. Giraffes
seekin more, necks cranked to check out the scene between
high branches of staccato, clipped notes of tonal tease.
The chimpanzees, with ease, please themselves with
eucalyptus leaves stolen from the pandas in pen ten,
grinning like Zen, and then some. With the pink flamingoes,
there goes the neighborhood. Splashes of cobalt in the zebra
stall, striped is all the hype, snipe some zig and zag on your rag
and keep the julep clippin on pursed lips and cheeks as big
as Dizzy's. Hip trippin move into the sax groove that taps
the hooves of antelopes and makes the elephants trumpet
along with the song. The lizards in their glass houses,
throwing no stones, cool blooded zone, slithering like an
eclipse of control and zippin to the electric buzz, the hum
of the tropical fish in their bubble. Stunned stingrays
and sharks roamin like vacuum hoses, their non-noses
over the turf searchin for snacks and attackin the backs of
fellow finned fanatics. In the attic of the club, those
chimpanzees trapeze to please the crowd, loud yawps
over the rooftops of the world. Hold on to your hats cats,
the tigers are sweepin the waterline with feline sleek,
benign to no rule and spoolin the line with jewel eyes.

Zoo you, Boogaloo. Chew the news, blow a fuse.
Dig that Noah with his twos.

Jazz

(listening to "Anthropology" by Charlie Parker)

indestructible oath of soul
core, honeycomb of pome-
granate, debut of magenta
nuggets of juice, bitter as life
and the sweet tang of livin it

fingers, lips, feet jivin
on the pile drivin dream of freedom
undeniable as sweat on the brow
in the pits of workin it loose

roll up your sleeves
this ain't no crackerjack
labor it with ebullience

a vocal focal point
fragrant as bayou sunrise
feel it in the guts
no third-row seat analysis

shake off the jockey
this ain't no pit bull
badass brain candy

note for note

a left hook
clean to the fractures
of inconsolable
memory

Blue Hues

(listening to "All Blues" by Miles Davis)

Miles drops
notes on midnight
like rain on misted grass,
tin roofs, the placid surface of a lake,
making ripples, expanding creative chaos.

Rhythm jumps in,
like a proud man in heat,
boppin down a city street, hungry for love,
laughin at traffic and the absence of fate.

Muted horn perfumes the scene,
hyacinth and tangerine,
a swift sample of Paris in Spring,
where they swing like Dizzy fools
breakin all the rules.

Newness and confidence combine,
an elixir of mind messin
sweeter than lime pie,
cool as a delta breeze.

The tease is the cat's,
without affectionate intent,
a marking of musical territory.

Miles makes the valves ache
for the tune, as catalyst,
not himself consumed
but consuming the listener.

Trust his line,
every time
you'll find yourself
fooled.

Off the Tip of Midnight

(listening to "A Night in Tunisia" by Dizzy Gillespie)

Wind the color of heat
Sweet scents of oasis grass

Water is gold
a man's only hold
on staying alive
in this sand land

In the cool night
the right rhythm
sends the horns
into maroon spasms

under a turbaned moon
beaming
screaming notes
careen through palm
fronds to stars
enough for a millennium
of gazing

Break into a camel's
lazing swagger

Carry the dueling
dagger of improv
to slice
a miracle
off the tip
of midnight

Piano sizzling
like a Casa Blanca brazier

Brazen flame
of saxophone
honing in on
the tone of tenacity

in the city
of enchantments

Salt Peanuts

(listening to Charlie Parker play "Salt Peanuts"
by Kenny Clarke and Dizzy Gillespie)

Bird blows
like runnin the Colorado

nothin slow

here we go!

into the stone's throw
from death row

row, row, row

your boat
stay afloat

don't gloat

turn it loose
like a mountain goat

highland notes
float like river spray

all the way

to the bank

laughing

Salt Peanuts
Salt Peanuts

Serengeti Sunrise

(listening to "Shooz" by Herbie Hancock)

Night seeps out, retreats
from silhouettes,
shadow puppets.
Birds preen, lipstick red,
slicker yellow,
chartreuse green.
Sheen on the sleek
neck of a sleeping jaguar.
Screams of hyenas
from a ratty pack
slacking into day.

Breeze scented of deep
musk and earth marrow.
Before the sun, the hunt,
the jump, the rump.
The gazelle's last breath,
the lion's teeth.
The steam of blood
against cool grass.

Jackal's eyes alert
in last moon, running
through stagnant dreams.
Blasphemous screams of elephants.
Mirage, distant image of water.

Light rising, dust devils swirling,
bits of brittle seed in fertile air.
In the first show of sun glare,
Darwinian dervish dance.

Set to Boil

(listening to "Locomotion" by John Coltrane)

In the molecular jive
the atoms dive and ricochet
this way and that
like Ella in a rippin scat.

Electrons spin like wild cats
tearin from their orbital norms
and slammin into the swing
of this hippest combo, H_2O.

Wouldn't you know
the show is just startin
with hydrogen boppin of the top
of the solid groove and makin
its move into a gaseous state
where the joint gets to steamin
and riffs are streamin like pure
heat off the street of dreams.

The kettle screams and the
hydro and oxy teams are dodgin,
diggin, loopin, hoopin, trippin
and rippin at the seams of form.

Bop is the top of the heap
when it comes to reapin
a fine line to blow your mind
and your own horn, scorn
the rule that says only fools
jive in where angels fear.

Tuesdays and Fridays

(listening to "Off Minor" by Thelonious Monk)

The gray garbage truck strains
down the still dark alley.
Two burly men in uniform blue,
sweat on pasty faces,
swing muscled arms, sling
dented cans, clear the old,
worn out, useless, rotten,
broken effluence of experience
into the groaning compactor
to crush into a square bundle.

In the grime of morning at five,
the beeping, backing truck takes
on a dumpster and rages,
heaving refuge, life's fodder
into its cavernous mouth.

The clash and clatter,
an urban thunder, shakes awake
the couple in their warm,
down-covered bed. Grating
on the brain, metal to metal
and the release of brakes,
the perfume of exhaust streams
behind, an industrial musk.

Spin Doctor

(listening to "Call it '95" by Herbie Hancock)

The bass drum hittin flat and hard like
a basketball dribblin along the court,
rapid and aggressive as urban ambition.
The hip hopity happenin groove movin
along the spine, as twines of electronic trumpet
blast past the ear, a sudden smear of clear color
across a canvas of slate August pavement.
Litter flying into the corners of the lot,
cyclone fence huggin candy bar wrappers
while rappers snap their tongues against roofs
of wet mouths workin loose the jive and the mojo.
The middle of the road ain't no place to be. See,
to be hip, to be in the pocket, rockin it, sockin it,
you need to step outside the mind.
Let the clank, chank, clink and riff of the raffy taffy
stretch a molasses mood on the tune.
The bass guitar booming in the lower register,
croonin like a moose and actin loosy goosy.
Ruffin furry feathers against the grain,
the keyboard's flippant flap, flip, slap, clappin.
Tappin your feet ain't enough, feel the rough,
ratty tatty splat of the mix, fixin to spin
off the fat like a lemming from its cliff.

Spliff. Splat.

Queen of Swing

(listening to Ella Fitzgerald sing
"I've Got My Love to Keep Me Warm" by Irving Berlin)

Living on the street, bittersweet child
singing for cash, a handout, a quick dose of joy
between long nights of New York's coldest storms
and hottest longing for something bright.

She enters the contest and wins first prize, but
being black, is sent back without the owed
chance to sing with the band in the white circles.

Her honeybee buzz pollinates the air
with carefree lilt, like she doesn't know
what she knows. It doesn't show,
her street-wise struggle, only innocence,
miraculously preserved, flows through.

Chick Webb thinks she's not pretty enough to sail
as figurehead on the prow of his swing show,
but her low, alluring, light and swanky jingle
jangles loose his prejudiced stance, and he takes
a chance on what she could be and becomes.

Cornerstones

(listening to "Well You Needn't" by Thelonious Monk)

This is Monk with a honky-tonk swagger
across the keys, loose wet, thick as a swamp,
but light as crow's feet on new snow.

Different from later versions, other hands.
Harder, more raw, salty, open, unmannered.

Fingers moving like rebel water over wicked rocks,
pleasing inner demons and packs of fallen angels.
Grunting all the while as if each note is born, not played.

The tune is short, curt and without solos.
Just Monk's mind monkeying, playing milestones

that become cornerstones.

Unexpected

(listening to "Round Midnight" by Thelonious Monk)

Full of furrowed edges and pathos.
A sour wine, piercing, staccato.
A blues of scathing, dissonant chords,
jagged punctuation, runs, arpeggios,
thrown like soiled clothes against the floor.

Saying, this is the road you've got to take,
unpaved, with the sun hot in your face,
or the wide night without a moon or heat.

The way we misread each other and ourselves.
This is the lament of unspoken apologies,
the sting of a sweetness we did not expect.

Audacious

(listening to "Giant Steps" by John Coltrane)

Iconic Coltrane
Brain wave altering game
shifting through three keys
to fascinate the eardrums
with tripster hipster slams
as notes percolate and gyrate
jumping in directions unanticipated.

A whirling dervish display
spinning beyond molecular cohesion
into pure light careening, a screaming
screening of the cosmic core

The sax untethered from its valves
the piano keys tumbling, a torrential downpour,
the drum swinging like a steel locomotive,
pistons punching, steam huffing, rails thrumming

Take these giant steps

Make the mental leap, eyes closed
soul opened, marvel at the madness
of these manic changes

Comp to comprehend
the mind bending blend
of free form and technical control

Coltrane racing past the finish line
a stallion tossing aside his rider
gliding like a rip tide to the horizon

Try to keep up!

Such head shaking impossibilities

Synthesis

(listening to "Killer Joe" by Benny Golson)

There, right in front of you,
the magic hovers in the air.

Thick, rich chords in hip syncopation.
Bold bass lines slapped onto a black canvas.

The horns just begging for your attention,
but coy, teasing, with a pretense of nonchalance,

waiting for your mind to open,
your thoughts to defer
to the stirring of the heart.

Wait, listen.

There, right there, inside this moment,
the mirror reflects you, truly,
as life spins its own tales
outside the lines of expectation.

Wherever the blood flows
secretive and sanguine
beneath the sheath of skin,
over the contour of bone and muscle,
the genuine pulse of life pushes.

Shuns definitions and sparks forth
from a subatomic need to express.

The rhythm of your mood shifts
in and out of dark and light,
day and night.

Entwined yin and yang,
balanced between the polarities
of love and longing.

Dancing their improvised tango
to the cosmic light show of chemical bonds
and electric currencies.

Breathe the brilliance of this synthesis.

Break from the mundane by crashing
through its simple disguise

to its complex surprise of beauty.

Manic

(listening to "Manteca" by Dizzy Gillespie)

Take that montuno
and pump it up
to go just so
wild

A line of horn
shearing the shores
of Cuba

Salseros
Congaleros
Chaos out of control

Roll the notes
like an Havana

Full and round
robust
grounded
in the soil
of African soul

Toil
with the tumbao
syncopated
bass line

add timbales
and heat
with habaneros

Troll the net
for the best catch yet
You bet
it doesn't get
any better

than Diz
and that Latin cat
Chano Pozo

Bolero Son

(listening to "Romántica Mujer" by Cachao)

Sound can be round
like avocado pits or
papayas, the pinkish
orange softness
of bold congas
poking around
like raindrops
on banana leaves
while the piano
weaves and comps
as parrots call
in poinciana.

Sound can be tangy
like over-ripe mangoes
lining sides of pot-holed
roads mixed with gardenia
and tuberose scents
lingering heavy
like regret
for things left
undone or unsaid

Sound can be sharp
clipped like wind
across steely water
the screech of monkeys
or deep emotions
playing hide and seek
the sight of Mars
on a streak of cobalt sky

Sound can be dark
like a mood
or a room
where someone sleeps
dreaming of islands
with names
that rhyme
with spices, liquors
and ancient occurrences

Phantom Cellophane

(listening to "Trinkle, Trinkle" by Thelonious Monk)

The experience of being
inside form, formulating the known
is less defined outside
the lines where rhythm schemes
seem to float as gin blossoms
obscuring principles
the good long spell of life
in the jukebox selection
the pedal pushers postulate
random idioms
self-indulgent jogs
birds of paradise lost
gliding cliff-side winders
What transpires in the mind
as it spins to oscillate the vibe
or to breathe as the alien tutu bird
flute chirps up the skirts
of the unknown universals
to a flip-side of fear
phantom cellophane
clear voyage to the pier
as in a long walk on a short one
subjugate the impulse
to gesticulate hate
riddle rivalries
guessing games of the charismatic
chemistry of subatomic fables
Cain and Abel's tables
of colossal cultural confetti
Free the debris from a meager means
and the meanness of a meaningless madness

Calif-horn-ication

(listening to "Boogie Stop Shuffle" by Charles Mingus)

Ancient impressions fingering
the pulse of matriculated matter
Ring the riot of love off the rocks
Relational rhythms schisms of schematics
The mathematics of cluttered attics
Remnants of inheritances
Slip through fences, subjunctive past tenses
Penetrate fate and free will wanderings
Enter, do not exit only
Loops, delays and echoed leads
Supersede the frantic filigree
Frescos of heroes
long ago dojos
Calif-horn-ication
vocalizational rehabilitation
Animated elation
Remains in the grain
to sustain the wood-shedding

Straight, No Chaser

People, Places, and Traces

Calliope

(listening to Miles Davis play "Jeru" by Jerry Mulligan)

On the carousel, your golden hair a swirl
over smile and glow, the pony mane's curls
flow in suspended memory of the eternal.

When I was three, just before the go
and don't return story, I must have known
innocence, as you do in this old photo.

Circling to the flow of Gershwin in organ tones,
a merry-go-round calliope, on the blue pony,
its sturdy, unchanging musculature set in stone.

All we really own is how we perceive the world to be.
Our past is known only in ghost form, and can you see
how only the future holds the brass ring's gleam as trophy?

Dos Gardenias Para Tí

(listening to "Dos Gardenias" by Isolina Carillo)

El campesino viejo plays his quatro, one tear in each eye.
In Vera Cruz, twelve white skirts spin to twelve white harps.
"Ay candela, candela, candela me quemo aé."
The Zapatistas move through the jungle's dark heart.

In Vera Cruz, twelve white skirts spin to twelve white harps.
En Tapachula, las manos de la vieja weave a textile rainbow.
The Zapatistas move through the jungle's dark heart.
In Honduras, dos soldados stop the Volvo.

En Tapachula, las manos de la vieja weave a textile rainbow.
Cruise ship tourists storm the beaches of Belize.
In Honduras, dos soldados stop the Volvo.
Tacos at Ernesto's, dripping with grease.

Cruise ship tourists storm the beaches of Belize.
"Dos gardenias para tí."
Tacos at Ernesto's, dripping with grease.
"Flight 950 to Miami, now boarding at Gate 3."

"Dos gardenias para tí."
The radio telescope in Arecibo hums to the stars.
"Flight 950 to Miami, now boarding at Gate 3."
A shop in Havana, the scent of cigars.

The radio telescope in Arecibo hums to the stars.
Baltazar carves dragons from Oaxacan pine.
A shop in Havana, the scent of cigars.
All of his children were shot in a line.

Baltazar carves dragons from Oaxacan pine.
"En el silencio de una noche azul."
All of his children were shot in a line.
Tenochtitlán under Montezuma's rule.

"En el silencio de una noche azul."
"It's too bad I don't speak Latin," said Dan Quayle.
Tenochtitlán under Montezuma's rule.
The hand of Christ on the cross with a nail.

"It's too bad I don't speak Latin," said Dan Quayle.
"Ay candela, candela, candela me quemo aé."
The hand of Christ on the cross with a nail.
El campesino viejo plays his cuatro, one tear in each eye.

Midnight Wages

(listening to "Goodbye Pork Pie Hat" by Charles Mingus)

Transparencies of old haunts and hangouts,
heat of New York pavement under slow feet.
The pooling of Venus beneath a moon, just off center.
Thinking about June spilling blossoms a thousand miles
across an ocean of forced forgetting.

Your eyes, one sad the other angry and full of harsh light,
as mists ooze over Soho like so many lovers breathing
in unheated flats over closed shops and noisy bars.

Placing the tone just outside of center
against the flat side of the note, as if the longing
for it might break your suffering,
crack open the oyster of discontent and
sneak preview the gloss on the irritant.

Two, three, four,
the one, ahead of the beat,
laid out like a fine table,
wine glasses waiting for the red,

and fingering the lace edges of desire
but not letting it register, just a guest appearance
just sitting in, just playing a hand, an elastic melody
that stretches over smoke and never settles

for less than your midnight wages,
rivers glide silent into a dirty dawn
full of nickel promise and the soot of dreams.

No thoughts, just movement by impulse,
a shark in churned water, snapping at
storm residue silting slowly below,

and then, the moon, and Venus
leaning her ebony elbow on a bourbon-soaked bar,
long, painted fingers against the lighter's edge
heading for heat with a too cool head.

After the Rain

(listening to "After the Rain" by John Coltrane)

Rain lighting on grimy window panes in April.
Photographs in leather frames of faces, smiling
from the deep past, flowers folded in untouched volumes.

The smell of fresh baked bread from a shop below.
The cat sleeping on the velvet divan, tail wrapped, a stole,
The way she stole your focus, laid bare your dreams.

She with fine caresses and silk dresses, cool to the fingers.
Her scented letters, read on mornings after sleepless nights,
after playing until the joint was as bleak as a sailor's future.

The corner that serves as kitchen, stacked with dirty dishes.
The deluge of a week's quick meals, eaten without appetite.
The festering worry that fingers will stiffen, be unwilling.

There is the woman in the upper flat with her sweet breasts,
but you would rather pine than satisfy this stoic hunger.
There are some kisses that stain the memory indelibly.

If the rain ever stops, you will walk in the streets at dawn,
pass the places one by one, taking in the feel of them,
the aching familiarity of the empty bistro chairs, whispering.

If the rain ever stops, you will stand by each fountain,
as on pilgrimage, and your soul will sing her odes,
but your heart will be a stone in the Seine, flat, reticent.

Paris Before Dawn

(listening to "Flamenco Sketches" by Miles Davis)

No footsteps sound along boulevards,
as street lights in puddle pools
reflect gilded dreams of angels.

The river moves imperceptibly,
a black snake under stone bridges
arching over centuries of history.

No prayers lift to cathedral ceilings.
Stained glass mouths of light,
now dark hollows to the stars.

Bistro tables hold their chairs,
legs spiked up into the night,
street gargoyles, horned beasts.

Even the thousand birds
rest in damp limbs of trees,
beaks under wet feathers.

An old man sleeps by the flower
beds, dark tarp on his legs, hung
over and chilled to the bone.

The roar of traffic, its ocean rumble
still a few hours distant, only a single siren
for a moment cuts the open sky.

A light in a window above a bakery.
Then the bakery lights too awaken,
and there will be bread.

Beneath the Surface

(listening to "Samba Triste" by Baden Powell)

I am more
or less

dominated
by a solitude

My needs
unavoidable
as yes

and as deceptive

In the night
we are minnows
sleek in silver lakes

We mirror
each other

in bright
and weightless
movements

glide silent

into that space

where air and lake
must meet

Troubled by the shadows
cast beneath the surface
of contentment

unnerving as doubt
We remain unanswerable
but embrace with such conviction

Jardín Rocoso

(listening to "Insensatez" by Carlos Antonio Jobim)

Her elegant shoes sleep under the four-poster,
covered with the settled dust of ancient histories,
luster darkened to regret, then to blessed forgetfulness.

She sits in the café until midday at the window table,
sipping tea from a porcelain cup, bringing to pale
lips Madeleine's and macaroons, eyes overcast.

Eldest of seven, hair once raven now a silver river.
Would-be actress, would-be dancer, dependable savior,
Courteous lover, keeping them all afloat with careful words.

White bird, sparing them knowledge of their own frailties.
Winging the family through its thorny gardens,
malevolent junkyards of temper in camouflage of luxury,
before the final, fiscal free fall.

Alder trees line the street, wearing their leaves at their feet.
Wind shuffles the bloom of their youth along gutters,
along sidewalks, as shoppers and mothers longing for sun,
expect sleet.

She has a rock garden beyond the old rose trellis.
Rivers of aggregate, gravel, conglomerate, breccia.
She has a secret, unbroken geode, an obsidian heart.

Seaside Lullaby

(listening to Miles Davis play, "Moon Dreams"
by C. MacGregor and Johnny Mercer)

Fishing boats lie silent, swaying in mild swells.
Lights slung over railings glint in opulent water.
Slowly the sea breeze meanders along peers
as harbor bells tinkle in a thin distance.

The town, sleeping now under summer's heat,
tosses this way and that in damp bed sheets,
making dreams rise like the tide under stars,
filling quiet ears with a light touch of guitars,
the strumming waves against silver beach sand.

A seagull flies, lands on an old piling.
The moon, smiling, hangs a crescent cradle,
elegant above a Venus nightlight.

Tonight, there are no evil men or wicked women,
only moon dreams and resting nets, settled bets.
The ocean's winking gleam steals all regrets.

Ode to the Clarinet

(listening to "Our Love is Here to Stay" by George Gershwin)

The clarinet,
the saxophone's
docile cousin.

Lighter of air,
milder of tone.

More conservative,
a terrier, not a setter.

Pliant but with a less
reckless passion.

Always on the border
of humor

but subtle.

Not the boisterous blare
of the trombone.

Or the hurly-burly blast
of the tuba.

The clarinet has
a more old-fashioned
finesse.

Folksy and wholesome.
A little Yiddish.
A little Turkish.

A little hurdy-gurdy,
yet tender

like a gentler man
retired from raging
complaining
or conquering.

Phoenix The Vegas Showgirl

(listening to *Lady Bird*, by the Jazz Messengers)

My name is Phoenix, just like the bird.
I like to burn, just like you heard.

But don't get nervous. Don't stare at the floor.
You see, this burning up don't phase me anymore.

By the way, you got a light?
Really, it's okay. I'll be all right.

My feathers are so used to heat,
I burn completely, head to feet,

without a cry of pain or sorrow.
You see, I know I'll rise tomorrow.

They say my ecstasy's a sight,
all billowing flame and red delight.

I'm learning how to do it just right.
Drink lots of fluids. Stay up all night.

I'm not a melancholy creature.
Depression's not my landscape feature.

I've been known to sing myself to ashes.
I've been known to laugh as the fire flashes.

I know this may seem strange to you,
but, Baby, burning up is what I do.

It's well rehearsed, anticipated.
In fact, I have accumulated

500,000 frequent flyer miles, and a large
supply of shuttle craft reentry tiles.

The latter were a bargain. Turned out to be a joke.
Resisting the fire only leads to nasty smoke.

Hey. That's my beeper. Gotta run.
Can I borrow your lighter? It's time to have some fun.

Swank

(listening to "Self-Portrait in Three Colors" by Charles Mingus)

Self-assured like a full wallet on a free night,
a good melody running through the mind,
a supper of steak, potatoes and red wine.

Self-assured like a young cat on a fence,
a round, white cloud on a windless day,
the weight of a Swiss watch on the wrist.

Self-assured like having the right names to drop,
laying the notes on the vinyl, in the groove,
a silver spoon stirring cream into coffee.

Self-assured like a coin landing heads up on the palm,
a fresh, red carnation on the lapel, a good crease in the pants,
a touch of aftershave, just enough to feel the breeze.

Self-assured as fingers moving over ivory or brass,
like minnows below reflected sunlight, or moonlight,
the breath that comes easy in sleep's embrace.

Self-assured like a man with a handsome woman at his arm,
a man with good teeth, an unbroken nose, a new fedora,
a man with a dream, not yet lost or attained.

Pintadas

(listening to "Barandanga" by Cuba L.A.)

Up on the ridge spine,
where the trail winds
between neighborhoods,
an electrical power transfer
station is ringed by concrete
adorned with vibrant graphic art.

The ornate iconic script
of streetwise Latino lingo rages
magenta on blue on black on yellow,
graffiti spray-painted over graffiti
to create a Mesoamerican temple
on the barbed wire crowned wall.

The mural is never static,
new skins of artful territorial
proclamation wax poetic
in flaming wings, burning eyes,
looping letters that rock and roll
to Old-School R&B cranked up
through lowrider Chrysler's
supreme subwoofers.

Immobility

(listening to Fred Hersch and Toots Thielemans play,
"Mussorgsky: The Old Castle" from *Red Square Blue*)

You wonder where you left your nonchalance.

And if you were to look again inside
the pocket of a long unshouldered coat,
you'd find it there,

a scribbled note
along the back of something torn,
of something half inscribed
upon your heart, a ticket worn and torn apart
to some embroidered symphony
of Bach, or Brahms, or Bartok.

And once, for you, the music held a dream,
now memory. You're sure she would remember you,
and even laugh, or maybe grace a tear.

But she, no longer here, is with her wine in some obscure,
unfurnished country, surrounded by an isolating luxury,
an ex-patriot living on the spoils of an inflated currency.

And you have failed in trying to forget her game.
You stop, uneasy, in the middle of a thought, and place
your unread book upon your chest.

You reach to close the light and hear
a car shift into first to make it up
the grade. That dog begins to bark,
just like it always does. It's very late.
You wait, perhaps expecting, what?

Eventually, you fall asleep.
You close your mind.
You shrug it off,
well seasoned Oblomov.

Jazz at Hoffman's

(listening to "Chelsea Bridge" by Ben Webster)

Sitting alone at a small wooden table
across the aisle from the well-lit desert case
in Hoffman's Bistro & Patisserie

I eye the pistachio-green crust on the Princess Cake,
the chorus line cream nipples of the hazelnut tortes
the golden marzipan rum rolls with cocoa lacing

The drum solo on *Chelsea Bridge*, rings lyrical, melodic
like the almost-black chocolate glaze on the elegant éclairs

A flounce and glitter of white Christmas lights dangle
from the proscenium of the thirty-foot window behind the band

The scent and taste of peppermint tea from a white cup
The bassist gently rocking his instrument like a lover

The pianist switches to a Herbie Hancock tone
cool and breathy as a Monterey fog bank

Braised chicken and roasted lamb over wild rice
served in the booths beneath posters of Paris in dusk light,
love sick dancers on the banks of the Seine

Ode to Chocolate

(listening to "I Fall in Love Too Easily" by Chet Baker)

on the tongue
bitterness
mixed with sugar
to appear sweet

density
mixed with milk
to appear light

chalkiness
mixed with oils
to appear slick

smoothness
mixed with nuts
to create crunch

dark powder
stimulant
aphrodisiac

a commodity
to siphon wealth
to the white

but white chocolate
is not chocolate at all

The Jib's Up

(listening to "Bemba 'e Cuchara" by Cachao)

With the salt sea slapping the hull in two, three,
four beats, your feet steady on the wet white fiberglass.
Sails taut with the wind, the jib billows like a slice of pie
against the solid blue sky, high above you
the pelicans fly in formation and dive.
The chop from the trade wind waves
arrives and turns the water rhythms
into staccato clave. The ocean
wide as the Mojave
and hot despite
the spray
you
sway
this
way
and
play
with
the
day

Pink Cadillac

(listening to "Take Five" by Dave Brubeck)

I am a 1959 icon, pink as the innocence
of a nation with a yet untainted reputation.
I represent overabundant prosperity, a no-hard-luck
charm, and the charisma that a few bucks can solve
any problem. I am absolved of responsibility,
even Elvis owned a hardtop model of me,
without worry about disowning his masculinity.
Clint Eastwood starred in a film named after me,
and a Grand Marnier cocktail hails my moniker
like a flaming flag in the face of the mundane.
Aretha, singing from my topless beauty on a pink
and white interior, was clearly a superior being.
I even drag-queened across the Bible Belt,
like a bottle-blonde Marilyn, with dirt devil
wind blowing across my chrome-edged fins.

Crossing the Golden Gate

(listening to "Blue Train" by John Coltrane)

Tiburon and Sausalito in bay brightness.
Chic boutiques, waterfront haunts and restaurants.
Entrepreneurial bliss, houseboats with loose
histories of rock stars and drug indulgences.

Leaving the Marin headlands,
slip in and out of slick summer fog,
the hiss of traffic through the tunnel,
hold your breath for a lucky wish
and leave the sun behind.

Suspended on the bridge, in damp
gray air, low clouds spilling over railings.
Steel cables painted brick red against abrasion
of sea salt air and ceaseless wind.
Suspending these thousand spinning tires,
spewing gold diggers and hippie pot smokers
into the city through her Golden Gate.

Brine water licks pilings of deep concrete
that entombed men for their construction.
Sluggish tankers and freighters, weighed
down to the waterline, proceed beneath her span.
Martinis at three on private yachts.
Thirty-foot sloops at full sail hit the chop
of the Pacific, tilting into the chilled wind.

San Francisco's high rise skyline displayed
on a silver tray of thick grey mist.
Coit Tower's fire hose nozzle rises iconic.

The Pyramid building's triangular tip glints.
Fisherman's Wharf swarms with tourists
consuming lobster, crab meat, and lattes.

Another summer in the city
of the *Summer of Love*.

Chaos Theory

(listening to "Better Git It in Your Soul" by Charles Mingus)

You are here, a red pin
in the swirling spin of the Milky Way.

Remnants of the Big Bang in your DNA
strands spiral around in profound perfection.

Every molecular rind in line
seems to define a master plan.

The mind desires order in order to feel safe,
while the heart seeks stars.

Reality is a fickle fabric of cyclical perceptions,
as beguiling as time and matter.

What matters most is the way you approach
the subject matter of life: like a challenge, or a joke,
like a riddle, or a mountain, or a landmine.

How easily it all unwinds at the first signs of trauma,
the crashing of dogma, the thrashing of new birth.

It's worth more if you savor the moment's
afterglow of contentment.

We are more than what we know.

Why do we try so hard to make everything jell and fit,
while life chews at the bit to run free of convention?

Kick ass!
Jump-start the steed of inspiration.
Attention! The tension is the juice.
Make it nectar, thick and sweet.

Meet the day with unmatched socks.
Shock a few habits to death.

Bang! You're Alive!

Death of the Bull

(listening to Billie Holiday sing "Strange Fruit" by David Margolick)

There are thirteen places left on the planet
where you can hear a pin drop.

Nostrils accosted with constant chemical confusions,
eyes red with residues of manufactured effusions.

The serenading shark's teeth of construction,
dissonant table saws, serrated brainwaves.

Five-bedroom monstrosities screaming into the landscape.

Complacency mazes unable to meet the pace of populations
racing to compete for the ultimate *Street of Dreams*.

Wake up tasting the aching memory of air.

There are only three places left on earth untouched
by the ravenous rumble of air traffic patterns.

Telemarketing sirens singing on the rocks,
"Buy and be saved from the truth of you."

But the truth shall set you free!

I've got God on the cell.
The roaming charges are killing me.

The moon is full because the earth is so empty.
Supersize the "Me First" mentality!

The missing twins of our capitalist
glory days haunting the skyline.

We are as free as canaries in a coal mine.

We watch direct TV while King Kong swats
the flies of fair trade off the Empire State.

We are Dorothy in a new brand of Kansas,
with the mini-malls and the eighteen-wheelers.

The moon will soon be full of people
living in domed Emerald Cities.

The weight of our credit card debt,
a gravity holding us to our grindstones.

Time is busy scheduling other appointments,
please leave a message after the beep.

The sharks of our progress circling the collective
consciousness like hungry stockbrokers
lamenting the death of the bull market.

West of the Moon

Ballads, Blues, and Ruminations

Facade

(listening to "Bonita" by Antonio Carlos Jobim)

If we cut away the fat
what remains?

Everything bloated with rain
shrinks in the heat.

All of the lifelines into
five-times painted walls

trace back need

to turbines
to aquifers

to the cataract eye of a star.

Only the surface color is ours.
I wash the curve of your back.

I watch the waves suffer,
not wanting to break.

Gibbous Moon

(listening to Charlie Haden and Pat Metheny play
"The Moon Song" by Charlie Mandel)

Where will you
be marooned
when the desert blooms
under a waning gibbous moon,
the prickly pear cacti
ripening her blood flowers,
as late July rain
settles and reflects
in impermanent pools?

Where will you bury your tears
when the last bald eagle
calls over canyons,
speaking the old language
into a silence
deeper than instinct?

Where will you park
your past-due dream,
like an old Airstream
wilting in shimmering
steel and aluminum
by tattered cottonwoods
under midday sun?

The Gila cliff dwellers
left behind their mysteries,
and their kitchens,

smoke-darkened ceilings
of dwellings where children
lay awake on winter nights
listening to coyotes sing
on mesa rims,
under gibbous moons
growing into full,
or waning into the horns
of the bull.

Where will you build
your sky kivas?

In the House of Love

(listening to "East of the Sun" by Brooks Bowman)

My eyes have seen the glorious scent of smoke.
The Devil's cremation in Los Angeles traffic.

Yesterday's rattlesnake skin shed.
A crumpled love letter from the sun.

My ears rumbling with love's confusion.
Disoriented as all delights go out at once.

It's not a love letter. It's a birth certificate.
As if you could be un-certifiably alive.

The state of the union is hecka plastered.
Billboard ads over ads, bleeding in rain.

We'll build a dream house of love, Dear.
The soft light of regret leaking through mini-blinds.

I felt as genuine as new leather shoes,
dancing on asphalt the color of worn midnight.

The new skin is doomed to become the old skin soon.
There is no place to hide the blue velvet past.

Carpe diem, wall-to-wall, rag, shag, plush, oriental.
The streets are rolling up their lush red sidewalks.

And the trampled love letters of brown-eyed bums.

We'll live in a lovely way, Dear.
East of the sun, and west of the moon.

Dolphins Have No Furniture

(listening to "Chameleon" by Herbie Hancock)

Dolphins have no furniture,
that's why they are so free.

Their children don't have bassinets.
Their voices sound like castanets.

Dolphins have no calendars,
that's why they are so light.

They never carry wallets.
They have no fear of night.

Dolphins have no signatures
except their carefree wake.

They do not own an oven.
They never bake a cake.

Dolphins have no mortgages to pay,
that's why they have a lot of time to play.

Dolphins never wear a watch.
It's always now to them.

Hocus pocus, cerebral, cerebellum.
Watch em skim, surfin on the rim.

More Sublime Need

(listening to John Coltrane play "Soul Eyes" by Mal Waldron)

Color is reflection of light not absorbed. Lime
is everything but, and tangerine's orange rind
is the estrangement of that very shade. Lately,
I wonder at the things not said. The weight we
choose to carry on, when there is no clear sign

and emotion bounces back off topic. I'm
not sure where the light goes then? In line?
In scattered fragments? Pieces of the prism beam?
Color is reflection.

If I can't adjust my angle of perception in time,
I may miss your meaning, or at least the more sublime
need you express between words. A theme
of longing for something I will never absorb seems
to be in question. How to hold and define
the pigment of love when color is reflection.

Blues in B Minor

(listening to "Welcome" by John Coltrane)

The river flows like holy water
through this city of brittle myth.

A gray dawn is no place for faceless
men wrapped in old news and plastic bags,
huddling under graffitied bridges,
waiting for the drizzle to ease.

No longer waiting with any hope
of a sweet salvation, only
waiting for another day to pass
without too much hassle.

The voice you once owned
won't go to its old crescendo,
sinking instead, deep down,
like a stone,
without a note
for a song.

Tailings

(listening to John Coltrane play his composition, "I'm Old Fashioned")

New Year's Eve and the old year leans in a corner,
champagne half-full in one hand, the other stroking
the velvet edge of curtains pulled against the glitter
from street lights and snow. The slow steps
walked along the avenue still echo with jovial
denial of the passing time, resisting the sting
of lovers gone and new loves fading
even now like sunlight into a sullen evening.

Midnight approaches like a train of thought
one can't hold at bay, keep away
from sketching some unsettling recollection
of how she never called,
and how the things she left
behind remember now her scent
and stain the remainder of these winter days
with hibiscus and jasmine.

The trumpet vines along the terrace
in the spring, dipping their blossoms
like tones from Parker's horn,
even the thorn of the rose had a clever note
to sing and who could know in that sweet
height, that things were cooling.

A thing or two you've learned
but not before returning to the coda of a sad refrain
all too stoic to name, and own the shame
of it in a face too pale and worn for joy.

Now the snow replaces lilacs
and the wind blows more minor
than Monk hanging on the edge
of the blues, and you've paid those dues.

The champagne is chilled, the company demure,
nothing rough is spoken, yet the festive mood
is broken by the tailings of regret and longing,
for tomorrow will begin another year
in which to find a final mending to this
endless ending.

Oklahoma Memory

(listening to "Sugar" by Stanley Turrentine)

He owned a barbershop, while
his wife Arlene ran the mom & pop
mercantile on Main until the Great

Depression came and leveled
dreams like a holy roller.
And dreams in pieces are hard

to glue together under the pall
of such heavy weather and dust
as thick as sorrow that billowed

in the acrid wind the color of rust
and penny cinnamon candy.
He became a handy man but even

that profession was less in demand
as everyone was fixing their own broken
lives and plumbing and raking their own yards.

All the yarns he used to tell about his wild
childhood ran together like paint in the rain
and the taxes and the bills came again

and again without enough on the table,
or to make the ends of their lives meet
together, weave together like a web of sweet

optimism that some day, not too much hope
away, he would have a place of his own
to hang that old barber pole, and his wife

Arlene wouldn't have to clean the houses
of those few remaining ladies of leisure
whose lives still smelled of lavender.

And That Is Enough

(listening to "Blue in Green" by Miles Davis)

Some journeys take place on the road,
asphalt rolling under hot tires,
a lone voice singing with the radio.

Skies stretch overhead like novels without endings.
Rivers cross under bridges crossed over at nightfall,
the rush and rumble of water and wheels descending.

Some journeys take place in the heart,
memories rolling by under dream gauze,
becoming more vivid under recollection's art.

Some journeys take us outward across landscapes
of deserts blooming and rain moving across plains
like curtains drawn, closing on the proscenium of escape.

Some journeys take us inward across mind scapes
of forgotten feeling erupting into our noon or moving
slow like the moon across plains of snow and maples.

I travel alone, my gas gauge reading near empty.
I take the next exit on this homeless highway.
Gas. Food. Lodging. The sign tempts me.

I travel in the hope of running into you again
under yet another disguise, perhaps wiser
than the last rendezvous and less ready to pretend.

I travel to ease the silence that haunts me,
to fill my diary with something more than introspection.
My protection is my movement, quick and stealthy.

I aim at the horizon without need to achieve it.
I dodge the obstacles of my trepidation.
Some journeys are for the journeying, if you believe it.

And that is enough.

The Love Tattoo

(listening to "Summertime" by George Gershwin)

Time listens, an old crow in the young corn.
Hungry. Patient.

Geraldine Maia Jones sits on the front porch steps,
her bare feet planted on the boards of the sagging stair
like they might never again stray from this place
of her birth. Her red dress sulks between brown knees
ankles swollen from years of travel and heels.

The molecules of wood under her soles resonate
with the vibration of the instrument at her chin.
The amber violin's sensuous form holds steady
as rapids of Rachmaninoff flow under fluid fingering.
She bows the white water tones into the windless sky.

She moans and pauses. The weather speaks Gershwin.
She turns her face upward into the full flare of sun,
her forehead glistening.

She adjusts the violin and begins to pull
the long, languid notes from the wood. "Summertime."

Silver Brown's hound dog howls
from its yard down the deserted Sunday street.
His chewed up ears hear overtones higher
than silent stars hiding under cover of heat.

The angels arrive, the old ones
who have been here for centuries.
They settle on top of the blossom-sown grass,
glowing like fireflies in the moist shade.

They rest their large, heavy wings
with perhaps nothing better to do
when good folks are at church
and bad folks are sleeping on their couches,
wearing yesterday's clothes and last night's
liquor on their slow breath.

The angels have come to welcome her home.
"We hear you, Sister!" they say.
Even as a baby, her mother declared,
there was no denying it,
"That child done talk to the Lord. See them eyes?"

Gera Maia has eyes the color of holy water,
opals set in the gentle mahogany of her face.
You can't just glance. You have to linger there.
Even if it is rude. Even if you do
get uncomfortable with yourself.

Those eyes can see straight to your secrets.
You feel them make you flush with the homemade
wine of shame, and grow lightheaded
when she's laying down a melody
because the notes are all the oxygen in the room,
and you have to breathe them deep
or swoon from the silences between.

It owns her, this music born in the belly
of her unanswered soul. She feeds it like a mother cat
takes her litter to her teats,
until she is emptied, sore and red.

She is a virtuoso. That's what the fat man said,
the second cousin of the Reverend White
visiting from Atlanta, wearing a suit
the color of elephant tusk and sweating
in the humid air from his own excitement.

He tells her daddy that Gera Maia is too good to waste
on some poor Baptist church off a dirt road in the dead
center of nowhere. "That child is a virtuoso," he says,
his mouth damp at the corners from the weight of the word.

And her daddy lets her go to New York on a scholarship.
Every Friday, a postcard. Miss Liberty,
the Empire State Building, carriages in Central Park.
Her mama carries those dog-eared cards
to all the neighbors' back doors
in the lazy hours of the afternoon.

Gera Maia doesn't come home except for summers.
She is full of talk then, hard to turn off.
So much water pressure she is fixing to burst,
so they let her refresh their minds with that fine,
cool spray about city life and music growing
into its own knowledge.

Like summer squash so big you wonder how
you're going to eat it all
and who you're gonna give some to
before it spoils. Everyone is like a child then, happy
and full of believing in something.

Gera Maia's mama cuts a magnolia blossom and floats it
on water in her best glass bowl. She lays the food out
on a faded, blue cloth in the grass,
shooing flies off the sweet potato pies.

Then it's Chicago. Gera Maia doesn't come home
but once a year for Christmas. "Too busy now."
Her daddy frowns, remembering about nowhere.
Voices rise one Christmas Eve to a place too tight
for resolution. Lights stay on late, all night.

Five years of concert tours. She doesn't come home
at all. Every so often, a post card. A quick, expensive call.
A lot of space between. Boston, New York, San Francisco,
Stockholm, London, Paris, Rome, Sydney, Moscow.
Eventually, just a distance without words.

But, Gera Maia is home today. Her fingers are buzzing
with it, with the being back at her roots. She turns
her spirit-water eyes to the old magnolia of her childhood.

It is past blooming. Tattered, cream-colored flowers
sulk between oily green and yellowed leaves.
She gets to her feet. Slowly and with effort
she moves through the thick silence she has suspended.
Digs her toes into the dirt. Stands heavy,
completely in the tree's cooling embrace,
branches overhead, roots below.

She touches the aged bark, her palm
on the marks she made when she was five,
her brother holding her hand over the knife.
That day, a fresh petal caressed her cheek.

Now, a wilted petal falls, glides down
in the still air, landing on her graying hair.
She feels its gentle weight, takes it in her fingers.
Touches its velvet to her lips. She leans back
against the trunk and eases into memory.

The polished maple of the stage at Carnegie Hall.
The first time. Her knees unsure.
The orchestra a tense net of security and expectation.
She feels the slick, cool silk of her gown begin to cling
to the small of her back. Alabaster to ebony.

The music is swollen with anticipation. She feels the taut
pull of her imminent entrance. She fills her lungs.
The orchestra falls silent. She drops her full emotional weight
down, into the bow. Down, into the strident chord.

Down, into the electric tension of the strings.
High. Suspended. She streaks the silent aural abyss
with the call of an eagle, the claim of a warrior.
A thunderclap of timpani and horns lifts
her solo onto the arc of a rising canopy of sound,
tossing her free into the giddy
atmosphere of Beethoven's ethereal mind.

Her diamond notes cut the glassy space.
She finds her grace over a rugged terrain of musical
theory stretched to its extreme edge.

She glides with profound focus over the glacial ice
of each delicate passage. She is so young. She is so new.
She could easily fall. She does not fall.

The remnants of her final notes are covered by an avalanche
of applause. A crescendo of approval envelops her,
the daunting embrace of three-thousand strange hearts.
She stands in triumph. She stands in tears.
She stands, listening to the roar of her achievement.

Is her father here tonight? She wonders.
She feels the abstract loneliness of fame
siphon away the nectar of her elation.

In her dressing room,
she finds a small, white box
wrapped with a pale, yellow ribbon
tied into a neat bow.
It contains a single flower.
A magnolia. Her mother's balm.

Time is liquid, fitting any mold.

An old crow calls
from the cornfield
behind the house.

Gera Maia rests her head against the fortitude
of her old, patient friend, her eyes full of inner rain.
She holds the withered, perfumed postcard petal
between thumb and middle finger, and returns
her forefinger to the tree's weathered skin.

She finds the letters there,
runs her finger through
the worn groove of wood,
the old wound, the love tattoo.

Circuitous Root

(listening to Charlie Haden play
"Spiritual" by Josh Haden)

not straight
to the point
to the depth

to the source

the source
is changing

is change

more like a river
seeking
curving

not direct
to the answer
to the question

to the destination

the destination
is changing

is change

not random
but chaotic
as fractals
are chaotically ordered

not unordered
but methodically
spontaneous

like feeling
the dark wall
for the
switch
for the light

feeling the dark
earth
for the rock
rounding
to the deep
water

the aquifer

the how
the why
the now

circuitously
found

No Ground

(Listening to "Ninety Miles" by Stefon Harris,
David Sanchez, and Christian Scott)

Where is the line between
what sustains us or derails us?

When do we walk off the edge
of our past and find ourselves

suspended,
momentarily in mid-air,
a kite severed from tether,
from guiding hand?

The flow of life is relentless
blurs distinctions of what feeds us,
what bleeds us.

When I wake up,
the sun is a glaring ball of promise

yet I wrestle as if a knockout punch
is the promise I've come to expect

When I wake up,
I stand at the edge of my past.

I jump off to find there is no height,
no depth, no falling

I spin and spin

I find no ground

Power Money

(listening to *Silly Putty*, by Stanley Clarke)

Power money is a muddied green,
oozing through the electronic screen,
rarely seen, always leaning,
pumping the consumer machine.

Power money is caviar on the tongue,
salt of greed, speed, seed of desire.

Power money is Wall Street noise,
the breathing of boys in labor,
spawning more, spewing war,
gun whore, environmental open sore.

Power money is high tech tease,
social disease, fees, the legalese
of fragmentation and decay,
chemical charisma and the corporate lay.

Power money is grown by the underfed,
bread-less, said-less flunkies;
consumed by the overfed,
Journal-read, highly-ed, Fed-Ex junkies.

Power money makes
heart fickle, soul brittle
mind cold, eyes sold
words hollow, wisdom callow
and everyone lust.

Wait!
Whose illusions feed
this shallow trust fund?

Subterranean

(listening to "First Song" by Charlie Haden)

Somewhere below the surface, where sunlight never filters,
and the forces are large, ancient and mostly subtle,
it takes a million years to make a change –

Somewhere beyond the range of sight and hearing,
a current flows like time outside of time and space
outside of space, a motion with a mute
determination and grace –

Somewhere remote from expectations
of nations and railroad stations
that things have order and are predictable,
there is the stone core
of what remains stable, yet unstable –

We move like mice and motes,
whole civilizations rise and perish
as continents push up against each other's edges,
creating Himalayas,
and even that takes a thousand ages –

We strive like a hive of bees
to compete and complete and be replete
with things like wealth and honor and ownership,
and what a trip to think that beneath all
of the conniving there is something grand –

and more profound that will outlast every clever blast
our arrogance may sound and remain untouched
by the minuscule rule of men –

A subterranean Zen –

Wild Perfume

(listening to "Dindi" by Carlos Antonio Jobim)

Ripples form the flesh of wood.
Petals form the rose's wings.
Rivers form so many things.

Kisses tease the softest guilt.
Shadows test the truest noon.
Beaches wait to swallow the moon.

Ripples of wood.
Petals of wings.
Rivers hurry so many things.

To barren silt,
To wilt too soon,

This wood, this wing,
This wild perfume.

Begin Here

(listening to "O Barquinho" by Antonio Carlos Jobim)

In the old Renault, bouncing on nameless dirt roads,
windows rolled open to the sea air, salted hair in a red bandana.

August dust rises in samba puffs off rear tires.
Sun's glare from azure ocean and noon sky in your eyes.

Shadows of pelicans flash over windshield glass.
Bare sandy soles against rusty gas pedal.

Oysters and scallops wrapped in newspaper and plastic
on the back seat, briny aroma of surf and morning breeze.

A song on dry lips, wordless and full of kisses,
as lithe lizards scramble from engine prattle.

Begin here, with the scent of gardenias,
the flavor of cayenne and coconut.

Begin here, with your eyes half closed,
your body tingling with the rhythm of clave.

Begin here.

About the Author

Eve West Bessier was born in the Netherlands. At age seven, she immigrated to San Francisco with her mother. Eve is an award-winning author of poetry, fiction, and non-fiction. Her work is widely published in literary journals and anthologies.

Eve is Poet Laureate of Silver City, New Mexico. She is also a Poet Laureate Emerita of Davis, California. She has a Bachelor of Arts in English and Creative Writing from San Francisco State University. She also holds a Master of Education from the University of California, Davis. Eve is a social scientist and educator. She is a studio musician, jazz vocalist, voice coach, life coach, visual artist, and nature enthusiast.

You can find more information, and enjoy performance videos and recordings on her website.

www.jazzpoeteve.com

www.ingramcontent.com/pod-product-compliance
Lightning Source LLC
Chambersburg PA
CBHW051657040426
42446CB00009B/1188